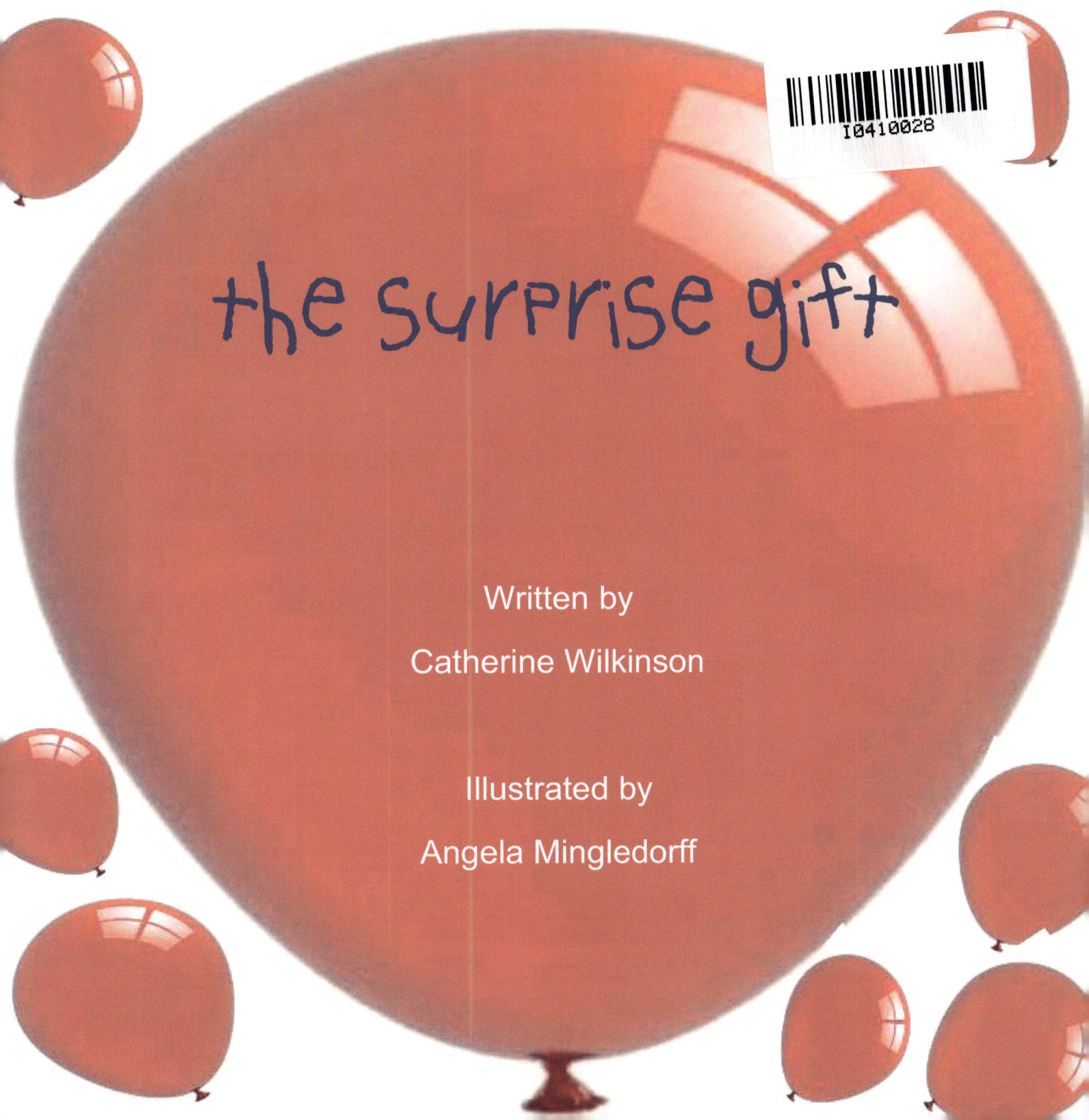

the surprise gift

Written by

Catherine Wilkinson

Illustrated by

Angela Mingledorff

DEDICATION

Dedicated to my little buddy Cooper.

ABOUT THIS BOOK

These books are designed to be interesting for your child. I hope that they will find it interesting to learn about the different emotions and things that they can see in their world. With these books and also the SELIA Kids program, my aim is to promote an introduction to emotional, cognitive and environmental awareness. Research has shown that a foundation in awareness can lead to better choices, decision making and problem solving. And that these can lead to a more fulfilling life for the individual and the people around them. Part of the importance of learning these skills is the practice of slowing down to become aware of and acknowledge what is happening around us.

Often so much is happening in our lives and our children's lives that children can get over stimulated and overly involved in the situation without realising. The danger in this is that behaviours can happen that are not healthy, or sometimes not how we would usually have liked to have behaved ourselves or have had our children behave. When we become over stimulated and bombarded with information, be it social, environmental, relational, or emotional, we start to lose the opportunity to think and make decisions.

Critically we lose the opportunity to learn the skills we need to live healthy and fulfilling lives. Often we don't realise we do not have the right skills to use within the challenging situation until we really need them! This is exactly what these series of books are designed to do, to teach your child and open the communication lines to develop strong social and emotional skills. Skills such as resilience, confidence, teamwork, leadership, self discipline, delayed gratification, and emotional regulation.

You will find as you spend time with your child with these books, and implementing the techniques, that your relationship with your child will change. You will notice your own understanding is improved, your child is more responsive, and your relationship will be strengthened. The questions within the books are designed to promote conversation in general, but also to set a precedent of your child feeling comfortable in talking with you about their feelings from a very early stage where your relationship is the most important one in their life. Please use the questions as a prompt, though expand and add your own experiences to connect with your child where possible. I hope that you will enjoy them too!

Catherine Wilkinson

BA (Psych)(Hons), Dip Prof Couns, Cert Frontline Management, Cert 1 Trainer, ...and Mum!

Today was a special day for Aston. His mum had a surprise gift for him. I wonder what it could be...

Can you see the balloons? What special day to you think it is?

Aston was thinking very hard, but he could not work out what the surprise gift was. It was a very funny shape that he had never seen before. It was pointy in some parts, and round in other parts.

What do you it could be?

When he started to unwrap the bright blue crinkly paper, he began to see what it was...

Can you guess what it is?

Aston felt so EXCITED to see his surprise gift was a brand new bike! WOW!!

What a nice surprise! What colour is the bike? How many wheels can you count?

Wow! Look how big and open his eyes are! And his eyebrows are raised and curvy.

Point to them. Can you see how excited He feels?

And his mouth is
open wide and
is a little smiley!

Can you show me
your excited face?

And he was jumping up and down very happily! Jump, Jump, JUMP!!!

Can you think of a time when you felt excited? What was happening?

Aston was very excited about his new bike. On he jumped and he rode around and around, and up and down the path.

What do you do When you feel excited?

Then mum decided they would go down to the park for a picnic and a ride on his new bike. There at the park was Aston's friend, Cooper.

How do you think Aston is feeling? How can you tell?

Aston was so excited to show Cooper his new bike! Cooper and Aston rode their bikes around and around, and up and down together!

What exciting games do you like to play? What friends do you like to play with?

SELIA KIDS PROGRAM

SELIA Kids is a division of the Social and Emotional Learning Institute Australia (SELIA). It is an opportunity for parents and carers to connect with their children and teach them the vital skills they need whilst growing in these critical stages of development and especially towards starting school. Skills for development that they carry through into adolescence and adulthood.

The Social and Emotional Learning Institute Australia (SELIA) was founded to establish social and emotional learning (SEL) as a fundamental part of child education. We operate a multi faceted approach working with families with children from 0 to 6 years through our **SELIA Kids** program, and working with principals and leaders from primary schools throughout Australia. Our consultants and program developers work with advisors in the United States, the UK and New Zealand to ensure up to date and established SEL practices.

SELIA is *Putting the Pieces Together* for child academic, social, and emotional education.

Social and emotional learning (SEL) is a strategy for developing the essential life skills necessary for greater success throughout all the different aspects of life. SEL builds the skills we all need to manage our lives, our relationships, and our study or work, more effectively and with greater satisfaction. Skills such as recognising and managing our emotions, making responsible decisions, handling challenging situations constructively, and establishing fulfilling relationships.

In respect of children, these skills help them to understand what they are feeling and make appropriate behaviour response choices that further help them to keep themselves safe and resolve conflicts or confrontations more effectively.

The Collaborative for Social and Emotional Learning (CASEL) has identified five core groups of social and emotional competencies:

·   *Self-awareness*—accurately assessing one's feelings, interests, values, and strengths; maintaining a well-grounded sense of self-confidence

·   *Self-management*—regulating one's emotions to handle stress, control impulses, and persevere in overcoming obstacles; setting and monitoring progress toward personal and academic goals; expressing emotions appropriately

·   *Social awareness*—being able to take the perspective of and empathize with others; recognizing and appreciating individual and group similarities and differences; recognizing and using family, school, and community resources

·   *Relationship skills*—establishing and maintaining healthy and rewarding relationships based on cooperation; resisting inappropriate social pressure; preventing, managing, and resolving interpersonal conflict; seeking help when needed

·   *Responsible decision-making*—making decisions based on consideration of ethical standards, safety concerns, appropriate social norms, respect for others, and likely consequences of various actions; applying decision-making skills to academic and social situations; contributing to the well-being of one's school and community

Please visit our website at www.seliakids.com.au

or for primary school educators www.selinstituteaustralia.com.au

ALL TITLES IN THE SERIES:

Elle Doesn't Want to Play
Aston's Building Blocks
The Circus
The Surprise Gift
Aston's Very Curious Day

www.ingramcontent.com/pod-product-compliance
Lightning Source LLC
Chambersburg PA
CBHW060810290526
45792CB00005BA/1591